SPLIT IN TWO

SPLIT IN TWO

Published 2010 by
A&C Black Publishers Ltd
36 Soho Square, London, W1D 3QY

Conceived, edited and designed by
Zest Books, an imprint of Orange Avenue Publishing
35 Stillman Street, Suite 121, San Francisco, CA 94107
www.zestbooks.net

ISBN: 978-1-4081-2815-2

EDITORIAL DIRECTOR: Karen Macklin
CREATIVE DIRECTOR: Hallie Warshaw
ART DIRECTOR: Tanya Napier
WRITER: Karen Buscemi
EDITOR: Karen Macklin
ADDITIONAL RESEARCH AND EDITING: Jeremy Bagai
ILLUSTRATOR: Corinne Mucha
COVER DESIGN: Tanya Napier
DESIGN AND PRODUCTION: Cari McLaughlin
TEEN ADVISORY BOARD: Atticus Graven, Carolyn Hou, Lisa Macklin,
                     Andrea Mufarreh, Trevor Nibbi, Maxfield J. Peterson,
                     Joe Pinsker, Sasha Schmitz, Hannah Shr

This book is produced using paper that is made from wood grown in
managed, sustainble forests. It is natural, renewable and recyclable.
The logging and manufacturing processes conform to the environmental
regulations of the country of origin.

Printed and bound in China by Wing King Tong Printing Ltd.

Split in Two

Keeping It Together When Your Parents Live Apart

Karen Buscemi

A&C Black • London

YOUR PARENTS HAVE SPLIT UP.
And whether or not you understand why
they're no longer together, it's important
right now to keep your own life on track.
After all, the most disrupting thing about
your parents' splitting-up is that it's...
disruptive.

This is a practical guide to help you through
the impractical situation of travelling back
and forth between two homes. Whether
you shuffle between houses every day,
once a week or once a month, the problem
remains: You are always in motion. You're
stuck in the middle, and your stuff is
everywhere. You can't find your textbooks,
much less your homework, and the diary
that tells you when your homework is due is
always at the other house. One step-parent
treats you like you're five years old, and the

other seems to think you're five years older than you are. Two sets of rules, two sets of responsibilities: one case of confusion.

In this book, you'll learn how to reclaim your sense of self, gain more independence and keep your head and stuff together. You'll find tips on how to negotiate with your parents to get things you need, as well as how to become a better packer, organiser, money saver and interior designer. You'll also read stories from others who have gone through the same experience and lived to tell the tale. The whole point is to help you feel less crazy and confused and more self-confident, grounded and whole: like a sane person living one life, not a scattered person who always feels split in two.

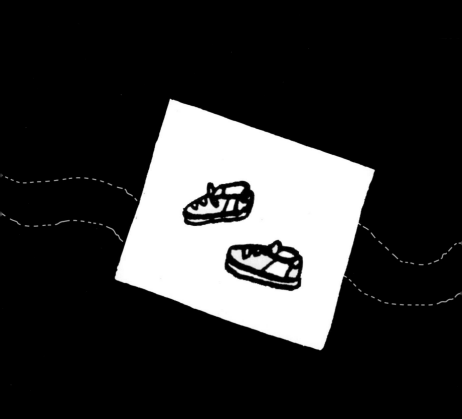

The Daily Shuffle

*Analysing Your New
(or Not-So-New)
Arrangement*

Your parents have split up, and that means you are trekking back and forth on some sort of regular (or irregular) basis. Living in two houses definitely comes with advantages (two lots of pocket money, one-on-one time with a parent and maybe even more independence), but it also comes with problems – as you probably know all too well already. Do you feel it could all work better than it does?

If so, start by looking at your present living situation. This way you can see what you've got going for you and what you're up against. See which of the arrangements on the following pages best fits your current situation.

Weekend Visits

You live with your Mum during the week and your Dad for all or part of the weekend.

Pros

1. It's probably the least disruptive arrangement, at least as far as your social and school life are concerned.

2. You don't need to have two sets of everything – just pack your bags and go.

Cons

1. It's hard to feel at home in a house you visit only at the weekend.

2. It may put a real damper on your weekend social life. (Your biggest concern may be fitting in your own arrangements without trampling on your parent's feelings. After all, your Dad has been looking forward to Jenga night with you, while you've been looking forward to a weekend at your friend's house.)

> « I feel like I have no one place to live. My home is always moving, so I never am really at one place. »
>
> DANI, 16

Every Other Day

You're at your Mum's house one night, then Dad's, then Mum's, etc...

Pros

1. If you really like being around both parents, this is the best arrangement: You are only ever away one day at a time.

2. The constant moving back and forth means you'll need a decent mode of transport. And that line of thinking could even land you your own car. Maybe.

Cons

1. Every day is moving day, and moving takes time and energy. You and your parents all need to be on the ball.

2. You really do need two sets of most things; other-wise you are literally living out of a suitcase.

« I am glad I get to see both of my parents. I have friends whose parents are divorced, and they never stayed in contact with one of their parents. »

KIM, 14

The Split Week

You live the first half of the week at one house, and the second half at the other. This means you'll spend some school days plus part of the weekend at each house.

Pros

1. This arrangement is a little less chaotic than moving every single day; staying a few nights at each house means less packing.

2. Again, you get to see both parents equal amounts, which is cool if you like them both.

Cons

1. You only have one weekend day (and night!) at each place, so your social life might get confusing.

2. Unless your parents are really organised, this can be a more chaotic arrangement. Both parents may forget who is supposed to be doing what and when.

> *To make transitions easier, make sure you do one thing consistently at each house. Every time I switch houses, my Dad and I go to the supermarket and race our shopping trolleys. I always know that will be a constant when I switch to my Dad's house.*

SOPHIE, 17

Alternate Weeks

You live at your Dad's house for the entire week and then move to live with your Mum.

Pros

1. You may feel calmer if you move around less, and you'll probably find it easier to remember to take the things you need with you.

2. You actually get to spend big chunks of time with each parent, which can be nice for bonding purposes – plus you have enough time away from each one to actually miss them!

Cons

1. You might also be away from a favourite pet or your best friend, making you feel homesick or simply out of touch.

2. Again, you definitely need two of most things – one at each house. You may be able to live without your Wii for a night or two, but what about the whole week?

❰❰ Because of the separation, it's easier to have good one-to-one relationships with your parents. ❱❱

NADJA, 15

Living in two homes is hard. You have to have enough stuff at each house, and getting to the other parent's house is time-consuming. It's also hard when you miss a parent while you're at the other parent's house, and it's difficult to have to split your time between your parents and your friends.

AMANDA, 16

Summers and Holidays

You have a parent living in another county (or country) with whom you only get to stay with at certain times of the year.

Pros

1. Being with that parent always feels like a holiday.

2. It's nice to have a change of scenery and get away for long periods of time.

Cons

1. You give up a lot of your social life (you have to watch your friends make summer plans, knowing you won't be around to take part in the parties and camping trips).

2. The out-of-town parent's house and community is like a foreign land, with no social outings (dinner with Aunt Ruth does *not* count) to fill your days.

I don't get to hang out with my friends as much as I did before because my Dad lives so far away.

ZOLA,14

What Now?

Does your living arrangement resemble any of those just described? Or do you have a whole different situation? If so, take a minute to work out the pros and cons. You've probably heard this before, but knowing what you're up against is half the battle.

It's great to know what *is* working for you and to acknowledge that. But it's also important to learn how to talk to your parents about what's *not* working for you. Next stop: Negotiating.

> *There is no time limit on how long it takes you to cope. There is not an exact timetable for everyone; people react differently to hard things in life.*

SOPHIE, 17

The Family Bargaining Table

*Learning How to
Get What You Need*

T hroughout this book, you'll be identifying things in your life that need changing and working out how to change them. But you won't be able to change much on your own. You are part of a family unit (even if it is not a typical nuclear family), and any small or large change you want to make will have to be approved and maybe even carried out by your parents. So what does this mean? You need to learn how to negotiate.

Negotiation isn't reserved for business people and boardrooms − it's something you do every single day. When your friends want to go out for pizza (again!), and you agree as long as they pick a restaurant where you can get a salad, you've negotiated. Studying with your best friend can be another chance to negotiate. If he's worried about the next day's algebra test, while you're dreading a chemistry exam, you can suggest taking turns at quizzing each other for 15 minutes. That way, you'll both get to grips with your respective material.

Your life at home is no different. If you want something, you need to know how to ask for it − and what you're willing to give up to get it.

10 Golden Rules of Negotiation

Lots of people are afraid of negotiating. They think:
What if I ask for too much? What if I don't ask for
enough? What if I annoy my parents and then get
grounded? But negotiation is less scary if you think
of it as a game you can learn to play. Large stakes or
small, the same rules apply.

1. Organise and prioritise your goals

Before talking to your parents about an issue, you'll
need to do your homework. Half the skill in negotiating
is preparation. To start, think about what you are asking
for and what you are willing to concede. Let's say you
want more privacy at your Mum's house, so you ask if
you can move into the spare room, which is twice the

size of your bedroom and gets very dusty. Are you willing to dust and hoover your new room in exchange for the switch?

Or maybe you feel like you are always broke by the time the weekend comes. Are you willing to do some extra chores to get more money? And will you ask for more pocket money or just cash for one special item? Determine these things before you enter the ring.

2. Be specific and ask for what you actually need

Say you've decided that your current curfew at Dad's house is way too early and needs to be extended to 11pm, as it is at Mum's house. Now ask yourself why. Do you want to spend more time at a friend's house? Need an extra hour to take the bus home from after school clubs or rehearsals?

If you start out with "I want to stay out till 11pm because Mum lets me," you are likely to get a flat-out denial or an arbitrary compromise; "Eleven is too late, but I'm willing to try 8:30pm." However, if you communicate the reasons behind your request, you may find a different solution that also works (your parents will agree to let you have friends over until 11pm, or they'll pick you up at 10pm and save you the bus fare home).

Just make sure you are honest about your needs. If you want to stay out later because you'd like to spend more time at your boyfriend's or girlfriend's house, but say that you need it so that you can study late with a friend, your parent may suggest having the friend over to your house. Oops.

3. Identify your parents' interests

You may know what YOU need, but do you know what your parents need? Have you asked? If you do a little investigating, you may not only see that your Mum's and/or Dad's concerns are valid – you may also come up with a solution that works for everyone.

Let's say again that you want to stay out till 11pm; your Dad has said 8:30pm. Rather than compromise at 9:30pm, or trade hours for extra chores, discuss the various concerns. If your Dad is just concerned for your safety (likely), then maybe checking in by phone every hour after 8pm and filling him in on exactly who you'll be with will do the trick.

4. Do some research

You've decided you need a new mobile phone/car/ spaceship, and you can articulate why (stay in touch with friends/be less dependent on parents to shuttle you back and forth/really need to get away from everyone). That's a great start, but you know your parents will ask for more info than that. How much will it cost? How will you (or they!) pay for it? What are the legal requirements? Do some basic research and consider writing up a document for everyone to look at during your meeting. The more information you can provide, the better your argument will be. Plus, your parents will appreciate your maturity.

5. Consider where and when to meet

Put some thought into the best setting for your conversation. A quick appeal as you're rushing out the door for school might be fine if the issue is a request for a few pounds to help you buy lunch that day, but not if the issue is getting a lock on your door to keep out a five-year-old stepsister. The more important the topic, the more you'll need to schedule a time and place where people can concentrate. But for less difficult issues, feel free to move away from the formal bargaining table. Relaxed conversations often occur during some other activity, such as cooking, fishing, a trip to a museum or watching a football game.

6. Decide who needs to be there

Think about who is involved. Want to borrow the car for a date on Friday night? You can probably work that out with Mum or Dad alone. But what if you and your stepbrother both have dates, both want to borrow the car and the idea of a double date isn't thrilling either of you. Or maybe you've found something you'd like to do over the summer holidays, or a job you'd like to take – far away from both parents' homes. In situations like this, you need to gather as a group.

It may seem daunting to have a whole-family meeting that involves step-parents and siblings (or even both of your split-up parents), but bringing

everyone together to face a problem can have great results. You'll find that there are more perspectives in the room to drive creative problem solving, and no one feels slighted or singled out as the enemy because they weren't part of the conversation.

7. Listen

One of the most important elements of negotiation is listening. That doesn't mean doing the "I sort of hear you, but I'm busy forming a response in my head" thing. That means *really* hearing what others have to say. Give your full attention to the person who is talking and ask the group to do the same. This makes the people included in your discussion feel that you care what they are saying; in turn, this makes them more receptive to your thoughts. Listening well will also give you insight into what will set off your audience and what will pull them into your corner. And you may even start to understand where the other people in your family are coming from.

8. Be partners, not opponents

The biggest mistake a person can make when negotiating is one of attitude: Instead of considering the other parties as opponents, think of them as partners in a group venture. (Which, strangely enough, is actually what they are.) Together, your goal is to find win-win solutions that make everyone happy – at least most of the time.

Work as a team with your parents. Doing this will allow you to learn with them as well as from them. I was angry with both of my parents for a long time for getting divorced. I thought it was selfish of them. But that only made matters worse. They needed my support and love, too. As I grew, I forgave my parents and felt extremely proud of them for overcoming an obstacle as large as divorce.

JEFF, 24

9. Stay calm

OK, you presented your case well, you heard the other party's concerns, you used all of your best negotiation skills and you still got an "I'll think about it." Whatever you do, don't lose your temper. That will only ruin your chances.

You need to really take care of yourself and make sure that you tell your parents how the separation is affecting you.

Instead, realise that an "I'll think about it," is actually a good sign – it's not a "no!" Also, accept that you will not always get an immediate *yes*, *no* or *alternative* offer. Don't expect to settle every matter with one discussion. Instead, expect to talk again, and stay calm and focused. Your parents want to feel as though they are making the best decision possible; let them ask questions and, if need be, sleep on it.

10. Be yourself

Whatever your negotiation, don't go in trying to be as tough as a *CSI* detective. Speak from the heart, be yourself and let your winning personality shine through. Your parents will respond more positively to lovable you than to anything dramatic or manipulative.

In the end, it's important to remember that you may not end up with everything you want. Some things you might get, but not in the time frame you were hoping for. And sometimes the answer really will be "no." For now. But your living situation will always be changing, and so will your parents' feelings as you get older. If you didn't get what you wanted today, don't think it was all for nothing. Some things take time, like chipping away at a big rock. Your negotiation today may have laid the foundations for a different one in six months. Or even six weeks. The most important thing is to have the conversation!

When my parents split up, they could finally be who they wanted to be. I also felt like I finally belonged and was an important part of the family.

SOPHIE, 17

BEST

(& WORST)

Split-in-Two Moments

KIM, 14

My Dad was driving me to my Mum's house an hour earlier than usual so I could go to the youth club. I was very grateful, because I knew he was giving up an hour of our time together to get me there. Then my Mum called my mobile while my Dad and I were still in the car and asked if I wanted to go to this haunted house that night instead. It was a place my cousins and I would go every year, and that was the last night it was open.

I really wanted to go, but my Dad got really mad that I was going to ditch the youth club after he had gone out of his way to take me back to Mum's early. I went to the haunted house and I had a lot of fun, but I felt bad for my Dad. I later apologised to him, and he accepted my apology and said that he would carry on taking me to the youth club each week.

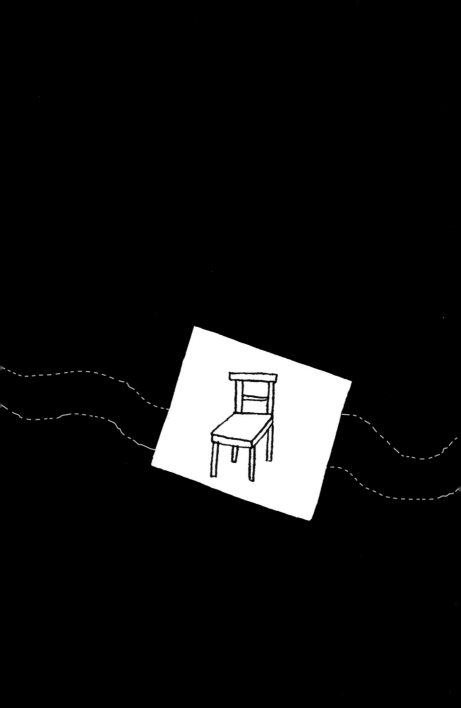

Your Room – and Your Other Room

*Making It
Feel Like Home
in Both Houses*

One of the most basic things that your split-home lifestyle can disrupt is your ability to feel at home. Before, you had one room; now you have two. And in this instance, two is not always better than one.

If you take a look at both rooms, it's likely that only one of them actually feels like home. That room is filled with all your stuff, while the other one is either plain and empty or decorated by a parent (or step-parent) who clearly appreciates a different colour scheme than you.

If you want to feel comfortable in both houses (and that's a necessity if you want to keep your sanity), you need to like (or even love) your living quarters. Don't fall into the trap of thinking the rooms have to be similar – they don't. See this as an opportunity to express yourself twice. One environment can be playful, the other serene. Or one may be cheerfully bright, and the other film-noir. Experiment with different accessories, different colours and different lighting. If you treat this situation like an interior design project, you can actually have a lot of fun with it.

« *The biggest disadvantage to living in two houses was losing a sense of home. My mind and body had to adapt to two places while I yearned for one base. It sort of felt like camping or hopping between hotel rooms at first. I didn't have one bed. I didn't have one room. I even had two toothbrushes. Each house had different soaps, different food, different rules, different everything.* »

JEFF, 24

The Basics

A bed, bedside table and a wardrobe is not a bedroom – it's a hotel room. Transforming that space into one that makes you feel comfortable will take time and energy. If you are moving into a new room, start with the non-negotiables:

Do you have a comfy bed and enough blankets?

Is the temperature suitable for humans throughout the night? Throughout the day?

Do you have a door, or at least some sort of privacy?

Do you have a quiet place to read/relax/do homework?

Do you have the basic furniture you need?

Any unresolved issues on this list demand attention from you and your family as soon as possible. Once those are all settled, it's time to explore some more personal options – making sure your music system is set up the way you like it, for example, or that you have the right bedside lamp so that you can read before going to sleep.

The Layout and Look

Where you place furniture and accessories can play a major role in how happy you are in your room, and even in how well you sleep. So can colour and light. If you need help deciding how to lay stuff out, you can google 'feng shui' (a traditional Chinese practice of creating good energy by arranging objects in harmony) or simply 'interior design' to get some ideas. Use the negotiation skills from Chapter 2 to ask your parents for permission and for help changing things around. And remember; there are lots of great low-budget ways to redesign a room. Look in your local newspaper for used furniture and spend a day shopping in your local shopping centre, charity shop or discount store.

Consider these tips when planning your rooms:

1. Your bed

Position your bed where it works best for you. Do you love to dance in your bedroom? Place the bed in a corner so you have the most floor space available. Do you like playing computer games? Move your bed so that it's sideways to the TV to allow plenty of room for you and your friends to sit on the floor, prop pillows and lean back against the bed while you play. Do you prefer symmetry and a room that has a more stylised feel? Place the bed at the middle of a wall and add bedside tables on both sides, with an alarm clock on one and a reading lamp on the other.

You should divide the things you are really fond of between both rooms so they both feel like home. Otherwise, you may end up loving one room and utterly hating the other.

WESLEY, 15

At first, I slept on a futon and lived out of boxes at my Dad's house. I also lived in hotels, as well as in several houses my Dad rented. Nothing was ever consistent, which is the only thing I really wanted, so it was difficult.

SOPHIE, 17

2. Accessories

Art is a great way to express your personality and make your room feel more personal. Whether you're into black-and-white movie posters or everything Hello Kitty, get some inexpensive posters, pottery, sculpture and calendars to make your room feel fun and finished. Place the art or poster you like best on the wall opposite your bed so that it's the first thing you see when you wake up.

3. The lighting

That harsh ceiling light is great if you've lost an earring or safety pin in your carpet. Otherwise, have at least one other light in your room that is softer and more relaxing. The easiest option is a small lamp on a bedside table, preferably with a low wattage. (But not so low that you need a torch to read.)

4. The colours

Colour affects your mood more than anything else, so it's important to choose hues that you like. You may not be allowed to paint your room any colour you want (though it is always worth asking), but make sure your room-accents (bedsheets, pillows, beanbag chairs, etc...) are in colours that suit you. Do you like nature? Go with greens, browns and cream colours. Want your room to feel soothing? Go for a range of blues. Like things a little louder? Add splashes of colour in orange or violet with a pillow, a piece of art or a patterned lampshade.

One bonus to having two houses is that I have two rooms and I get double the stuff.

TRAVERS, 17

Yours, Mine and Ours

Not enough bedrooms to go around? If you have no choice but to share, never fear. You can bunk with a sibling and still make your room feel like your own.

Your negotiation skills will again be helpful here. To start, have a sit-down with your roommate and decide on a design theme you both like. Keep an open mind about different ideas and how you can incorporate your personality into the décor. For example, say you want every inch of the room dripping in pink, but your sister is set on a sports theme, which doesn't inspire you at all. You can compromise on a beach theme, where your sister gets elements of surfing and beach volleyball, while you can add big (pink!) sunglasses, a beach umbrella and bikini-printed pillows. If you get along well enough, this can be a great opportunity for artistic collaboration.

The other option is to have a clear separation of sides. You decorate your side the way you like, while your sibling decorates the other side in his/her own way. This can often work out fine as long as you come to agreements on who gets what wall space, floor space and wardrobe space. When in doubt, measure things to be 50-50. Maybe even hang up a beaded, bamboo or fabric curtain that can be closed if either of you wants privacy. Remember, you're going to be spending a lot of time together in this room, so start off on a positive note, working together and being flexible enough to make a change or two so you're both happy with your finished space.

Staking Out Your Territory

Let's face it, no one wants people wandering into their room uninvited and looking through all their stuff. And while that may not have been a problem before, everything changes when you add new step-parents and siblings into the mix. If you find yourself sharing a home with new people, use your communication and negotiation skills to call a family meeting to discuss privacy and respect for each other's things. Be sure to cover the differences between asking and assuming, borrowing and browsing. Get everyone involved in making some ground rules so no one feels picked on. This process isn't foolproof, but it's a good way to start.

If you're sharing a room, you need to arrange times of the day when you can be guaranteed some time alone to relax, do homework or talk on the phone. For example, on weekdays from 5–6pm, you get your room to yourself while your sibling gets it from 6–7pm.

Remember that your room is more than just a space. It's a big part of your life. If you like where you live and sleep, you've won half the battle.

I'm Supposed to Be Where When?

Dealing with Your Crazy Schedule

Everyone has a crazy schedule these days. But navigating a busy life is harder to do when your time is split between two houses – especially if one is a long way from your school, your friends or your job. Not knowing where you are supposed to be, and when, is stressful, for both you and your parents. It can also make you feel disorganised.

Getting organised may sound less than exciting, but it's true what people say; with structure comes freedom. Once you have a system in place, you'll be less focused on the minute-by-minute chaos of your life and more able to concentrate on important things – like school, a new boyfriend/girlfriend, or how to win the football game. Organisation also equals more independence. You can schedule your time better if you actually know what your weeks – and your parents' weeks – look like in advance. This will also help you work out ways to get from A to B more easily.

With the right tools and skills, and a little practice, you may soon be even more organised than your parents.

> « *Living in two homes makes organising school stuff extremely difficult. I often have to make trips back and forth from my Mum's house to my Dad's house on weekdays just to grab a folder or something, and I realise that's not even possible for a lot of kids. I think my school work has suffered, and I haven't worked out how to balance it all out yet.* »

MAX, 16

Choosing a Calendar System

First things first, you need a calendar. There's just too much stuff going on to keep track of it all in your (or your parent's) head – and forgetting about a tennis game, gig or school trip might involve a 6am emergency trip to your other house for your stuff. A good calendar will ensure you have the things you need for the next day, the next week and even the next month.

Decide on the calendar that works best for your situation, and make sure your important dates are bold and central. There are three basic types of scheduling devices you can use to keep track of yourself (and your parents). You may find that you need to use only one or you might need a combination of some or all of them.

1. Internet calendar

If you have Internet access at both houses, using some type of web-based planner is probably the best method for keeping track of schedules for both you and your parents. There are many web-based calendars out there (Google, Yahoo, Microsoft), and most of them are free. This is an amazingly easy way to keep track of who's taking you to the dentist, who's driving you to the school disco (which you now may want to skip) and who's picking you up from rehearsals.

The bonuses of using an online calendar:
1. It can be shared between all three of you (as well as any siblings and step-parents who are in the mix). That means you and your parents can add or edit events as

needed, without the need for text messages, voicemails, or sticky notes. (This method also turns out to be extremely helpful if Mum and Dad aren't communicating well offline.) For extra clarity (and flair), use a different colour for each person's schedule.

2. You don't need to have an online calendar with you. You can access it from any computer anywhere.

3. You can use an online calendar to remind yourself about stuff. Send notes to yourself: "Remember to pack uniform for Sunday's game," or "Don't forget to e-mail Dad the school picture payment info." With some software, you can even send those reminders to your e-mail or mobile phone.

4. You can be as public or private as you want. Share parts of the calendar with your parents and keep your own stuff private. This is great when you want your parents to see where to pick you up on Thursday, but not the phone number of the guy/girl you called on Friday.

To find the best Internet calendar for you, do an online search, check out what each has to offer and select the one that suits your needs. Then prepare yourself for the real challenge, teaching your parents how to use it. If they are computer savvy, you're in luck. If not, plan a few 15-minute tutoring sessions. Short learning sessions generally work better than long ones in which your parents stare at the computer screen quizzically in between yawns. If you write down a step-by-step list of what to do, your Mum and Dad will be especially grateful.

2. Jumbo wall calendar

If your parents are not technologically savvy, or just generally like to have things right in front of their faces to help remind them of stuff, a large paper or dry-erase calendar is a great option.

The bonuses to using a jumbo calendar:
1. It's available at all times, even when your computer is off. You, your Mum or your Dad can write something on it as soon as they walk in the door, and you can leave them reminder notes to feed your fish while you are away.

2. A wall calendar serves as a constant reminder. Every time you walk into the kitchen, living room or wherever you've decided to hang it, you can't help but see it. If something lives only on your Internet calendar, you have to actually remember to check it; with a wall calendar, you can't miss it.

Co-ordinating Mum's and Dad's wall calendars is the only tricky part here, otherwise you'll end up with calendar chaos! Keep everyone's calendar updated or have a web-based calendar and/or keep your own portable planner as a backup.

Living in two homes is really hard in any situation. It is important to take a deep breath and organise yourself.

DANI, 16

3. Portable planner

This method is great for people who like to have their schedule with them at all times. It's also a great supplement to both a jumbo calendar and an Internet calendar. Blackberries and some mobile phones can serve as personal planners, but bear in mind that they can run out of battery or crash – things that paper planners won't do.

The bonuses to using a portable planner:

1. It's portable. Plain and simple. You can toss it in your rucksack or handbag, and write info down the moment you find out about it – whether you're online or not.

2. It's personal. It's for your eyes only. You can keep all of your private stuff in here (social, academic or whatever), and just transcribe the stuff your parents need to know onto the Internet calendar or jumbo calendar when you get home each day.

No matter what kind of planner(s) you choose, make sure that you and your parents come up with a system for maintaining them. Do your best to make sure that all the relevant info is getting to all of the parties involved. Every family is different, so work out what is best for all of you.

What Gets Written Down

Once you have decided which method you are using,
you'll need to work out what goes on the calendar(s).
Here are three general categories to consider.

1. Basic events

This is the everyday, regular stuff, all of which needs
to go on the calendar: practices and games, work,
appointments, study groups, parties, holidays, concerts,
shopping trips and family events. Also, ask your parents
to add everything they have going on that might affect
your schedule.

2. Transport

You know where you want to be, but how will you get
there? Is a parent willing to drive you? Can you borrow
the car? Or do you need to find another way (friend,
bus, bike, tractor)? Make sure you note travel
arrangements on your calendar, and get the relevant
parties to sign off their approval. You don't want to
find yourself stranded when you're supposed to be
at the front row of a long-awaited pop concert.

3. Parental play time

It might not seem like a big deal to you to ditch your Mum's Scrabble night for a friend's party, but she may have spent the last week memorising words that start with 'X' for her evening with you. If your parents want to spend time with you, take them up on it! To prevent parental time from interfering with your social life, make an appointment on the calendar – and not on nights when you have a hot date or a big party.

> « My family and I keep a planner that has all the things I need to do, which house I will be at and who will be picking me up. That way we can all stay on the same page. »
>
> WESLEY, 15

Managing Your Time

In a life full of schoolwork, homework, sports, artistic pursuits, a social life and family obligations, it's hard enough for anyone to manage his/her time. But if you live in a split-family situation, your obligations can feel like they are doubled or tripled. For one thing, both of your parents see you less than they did before, so when you are around they want to spend more of that time with you. In addition, you now need to factor in separate time to spend with your Mum's new romantic partner and your Dad's family and friends.

This is why you probably feel at times that everyone wants to be with you – and that you are not free to have a life of your own. Maybe your Dad really wants you to hang out with him and his new girlfriend this Saturday. Then your Mum says she wants to take you to meet her new husband's family on Sunday. Great, but what happened to your own weekend?

With all these demands, it's important to manage – and protect – your own time. That means doing your best to see all of the people your parents want you to see and also knowing when to ask for a 'get out of jail free' card (which may actually be a 'get out of dinner with your step-parent's sister-in-law free' card). Instead of miserably agreeing to all demands – or always retorting with a flat-out 'no', have a discussion with your parents about how much family time they can each reasonably expect of you. Remind them that you're now dividing your total family time between two sides, so each side will actually get to spend less time with you.

This kind of negotiation, by the way, will continue with your family well past school.

> *It can be very hard to plan my time because I always have to take into account which house I will be going to or coming from and how much time it will take. It can sometimes be quite annoying when I realise I won't be able to do something because I can't make it home in time.*

WESLEY, 15

Dividing Special Occasion Time

Having parents who have split up gets more complicated around special occasions. Mum and Dad could both have plans for you that you might not even know about until the last minute, when you discover you're double-booked. Here are some suggestions for dealing with school and university holidays, birthdays and trips away.

1. School and university holidays

In split families, celebration navigation becomes an art. How holidays are handled will depend on how many people are hosting, the timing of the events and where houses are located. For example, if your Dad's Uncle Jim is having Christmas dinner on his farm at 3:30pm, and your Mum's Aunt May is planning a similar feast at her flat in the city at 4pm, there's obviously no way you're going to make it to both events (and your stomach may thank you for that). Chances are, your parents will decide which event you're attending, so if you were looking forward to feeding the chickens at the farm, you'll need to speak up.

However, if one side of the family is sitting down for a meal in the early afternoon, while the other is planning an evening feast, you can realistically plan to spend the holiday with both parents. Just make it clear that Grandma shouldn't feel upset if you've already eaten a plateful of food at the earlier dinner and don't want to indulge a second time. No one has to pile on the pounds trying to please everybody.

As you can imagine, sorting all of this out takes some negotiation between your parents (help them out with what you read in Chapter 2). In some families, Mum's (or Dad's) side will agree to celebrate Christmas (or Hanukkah or whatever) a day later to accommodate everyone's needs. In the end, the holidays are more about being together than celebrating on an exact date. If your parents lose sight of that, don't hesitate to remind them.

2. Birthdays

For birthdays, you have a few options. One parent takes the day, the other takes the evening. Or maybe one parent takes Saturday, and the other takes Sunday. Or maybe you want to hang out with your friends instead. It's your birthday, so it's really up to you. Of course, this is also a great opportunity to stretch your birthday into a birth-week and have three or four times as many celebrations as you would normally have – if your family goes in for that sort of thing.

> ❝ The best part of my parents' splitting up was having two of everything. Christmases, birthdays, beds, bikes. And then I eventually got two new step-parents who have been a major influence in my life. ❞
>
> KELSEY, 19

In the early years of my parents' divorce, my Dad would come to my Mum's house, and we would still all get together for Christmas and my birthday. But when my Dad met someone else, that all changed. We had to plan two Christmases and two birthdays.

I thought that moving away for university would help, but it did the opposite. When I would come home for the weekend, I had to make a complete schedule for which houses I would stay at and when, bouncing around all weekend to see everybody. I couldn't just relax and go with the flow.

JEFF, 24

I hate having to go back and forth on the same day on holidays to spend time with both parents.

AMANDA, 16

3. Trips away

Booking trips away generally creates fewer conflicts, unless both parents want to whisk you away for half term, which is unlikely. Now that you have a calendar system that works, use it to ensure that your family holidays away don't interfere with each other or with a social event you were planning to attend. If there is a conflict, talk to your parents about it calmly. It's hard to be excited about a holiday when you know that you're missing out on something else big.

If you're at your Mum's house, sometimes you miss something that happens that weekend with your friends because you are hanging out with your Mum.

AMANDA, 16

Whatever your preferences for school and university holidays, birthdays, and trips away, be sure to voice your opinions far enough in advance so that your choices can be worked into each family's plan. No one will know what you want unless you speak up.

And when talking about a holiday with your parent, consider this: It could be fun to plan a short trip for just the two of you. Big family holidays with siblings, a new step-family or a parent's significant other can be fun, but it's important to keep close bonds with your parents, too. Invite your Mum or Dad on a trip to see your favourite football team play in another city, a hiking trip in the hills or a theatre visit or spa weekend. Now that your parents are no longer a unit, you may get to know them on a whole different level than you would have if they had stayed together.

One of the advantages of having divorced parents is that you start to notice the distinct personality of each one, whereas when they're together, their personalities may blend. Now you have a really separate relationship with each parent, so your Mum's or Dad's unique personality and way of life is more apparent – and you can start to bond with that new side of them.

JOSH, 20

The Life of an Intrepid Traveller

Learning How to Pack and Haul It All

If you're living in two homes, you are probably becoming the queen or king of packing. It can be a complete pain at times, especially when you forget things (such as homework or a favourite book or DVD) at the other house. Constant re-packing can also make you feel pretty disorganised, unsettled and even exhausted.

But there is an art to packing and hauling stuff around, and mastering that art can help you go from feeling like a homeless tramp to an intrepid traveller. A good packing system can help you pack efficiently and quickly and also help keep your breakables safe, your clothes in pristine condition and your stuff more or less condensed and portable. Knowing what and how to pack is a skill you will use your entire life, making you a better, more easygoing and more flexible traveller.

BEST

(& WORST)

Split-in-Two Moments

BEN, 17

Once I was having a sleepover at my Dad's house and, like every good sleepover, it needed an Xbox, which was (not so conveniently) at my Mum's house. I left a pleading message on her phone to bring it over, but when she didn't reply for half an hour my phone died, and my friend and I decided to take the bus over to her house. By the time we got there, she had received our message and had driven the Xbox over to my Dad's house, leaving us to take the 45-minute trip back again. After that we were so exhausted we barely played any video games at all.

10 Tips to Help You Get Your Packing Act Together

1. List it

Before you start packing, make a list of what you need. This will save you from the agony of discovering you left behind a beloved band T-shirt or favourite squishy pillow. Take your time putting this list together, so when you begin to pack, you don't randomly throw "I might need these," items into your bag and forget the "I should have packed those," items altogether. Don't forget to include the ever-important chargers for your mobile phone, laptop, iPod and camera! Tick off the items on the list as you place them in your bag, and save the list somewhere that will be easy to access – in your diary or on your laptop – no matter where you are.

Make sure you have the necessities at both houses. I used to have a checklist that I would look at so I could make sure I had my homework and clothes and stuff... One time I forgot my computer power cord at my Dad's, so I couldn't use my computer for a week.

TRAVERS, 17

2. Lighten up

The less you pack, the easier your trips between houses will feel. The easiest way to pack fewer clothes is to stick to a small colour palette so everything matches. Also, select clothes that layer well, so you don't always need to bring bulky jackets. Pack mini-bottles of your toiletries and cosmetics instead of dragging super-sized shampoo or shaving cream bottles back and forth. (Or just have two sets of toiletries – one for each house.) Keep your school books in a separate rucksack so they don't squish your clothing.

3. Think small

Buying something for yourself? If it's something you will want to bring with you when you change houses, consider going with the most compact model or with gadgets that serve more than one purpose. For instance, a laptop with a built-in DVD player eliminates the need to drag around a portable DVD player. Also, a thinner, smaller laptop is easier to haul around than a big clunky one. Anything that lightens your load will make shuffling between houses a more pleasant experience.

4. Avoid wrinkles

Rolling your clothes tightly can save room *and* prevent wrinkling. For trousers, fold in half lengthwise and then roll. For shirts, fold back the sleeves and then roll. Remember, less folding equals less wrinkling.

It seems like, no matter what, all my boxers end up at one house, and all my socks at the other. There's really no way I can think to control this, especially because the structure of what night I stay at what house is never the same, and it all becomes really sporadic.

5. Make space

Consider using vacuum seal bags (available at most good travel shops and on the Internet); to let you compact your clothing so it takes up less space. This is especially useful when you visit one parent for a month or longer.

6. Create order

When using a suitcase, pack bulkier clothing items at the bottom, with the most delicate clothing on top, and make sure breakable items are cushioned by woolly jumpers or pajamas somewhere in the middle. If you're using a rucksack, place softer, lighter items on the bottom and put the heavier items, including toiletries, on top. (Putting heavier items higher up on your back and closer to your body decreases the chance of lower back strain.)

Always make sure you have everything you need before switching homes. Sometimes I'd leave my mobile phone charger, homework or school shoes at one house, and neither parent is willing to get them.

DANI, 16

7. Use shoes

Place underwear and socks (and any other small objects) inside shoes to save room. Pack shoes by either facing the tops of them towards each other, heel to toe, which creates a rectangular base on which you can stack other items, or place them around the edges of your suitcase.

8. Stay dry

Put as many liquid toiletries as possible into small travel containers. Sets of these containers are easy to find at the chemist; the kind made for air travel are especially good, even if you are only travelling on the ground. Keep these containers in a closed toiletry bag so you don't wind up with hair gel in your boots. (Yuck.) Stock up on sealable bags and use them!

9. Stay organised

Keep things separated either by compartment or by when you will need them (things you need sooner go on top). To keep your smaller items separated and easy to find, use travel organisers, such as a jewellery case (available at most travel shops) or sealable bags. Have a separate rucksack for your school stuff, and always double-check to make sure you've got everything you need before you leave the house.

10. Leave a little extra space

It's possible you'll return with more than you left with. Just one shopping trip can push your suitcase to its limit. Either leave enough room in your luggage for new items, or pack a collapsible bag that can turn into rucksack number two if you need it.

The Bag You Drag

You'll need a proper bag (or bags!) for items you will be hauling between houses. A rucksack is great if you switch houses every other night. If you take a laptop back and forth, get a rucksack with a built-in laptop compartment. Longer-term haulers might want to opt for something with wheels, especially if your stuff feels heavy, or a duffel bag if you want something you can swing over your shoulder and carry easily up and down stairs. If one bag feels too heavy, divide your stuff between two smaller bags; they'll wedge more easily into Mum's or Dad's car – and be easier to heave in and out.

Make sure you get doubles of your favourite jeans so you can keep a pair at each house.

SOPHIE, 12

Make Yourself Comfortable

Once you get home (whichever home that is), take a few minutes to unpack. It may be tempting to live out of your bag or suitcase, especially if you'll only be there for a few days. However, having your things in drawers and your clothes hanging up in the wardrobe will make you feel more at home and less like a hotel guest. It will also help you find your stuff more easily and without making a mess. And don't forget to reuse that packing list when it's time to pull all your things together again. After a while, you'll notice that packing becomes second nature.

It's important to unpack my stuff, because it helps me feel more organised, and it also helps my room feel more like home.

WESLEY, 15

BEST
(& WORST)
Split-in-Two Moments

AMANDA, 16

My Dad lives about 30 minutes away from my Mum's house, which is where I live most of the time. Every other weekend I go to my Dad's house. One weekend, I brought my tennis shoes to my Dad's – a red pair and a black pair – so I could leave one pair there permanently. On Sunday night, when I was leaving my Dad's house, I packed my shoes. When I was getting dressed Monday morning at my Mum's house, I put on my shoes – but I didn't realise until I got to school that I was wearing one red shoe and one black shoe. I had mixed them up.

Cash Control

Creating Some
Financial Independence

One way to feel more in control of your split-in-two life is to exercise some control over your finances. For many kids in split families, the equation is simple: Money equals freedom. Freedom to buy those things that both of your parents keep saying the other one should buy you; freedom to go out at the weekend or get that new pair of jeans despite the fact that your parents are feeling strapped for cash due to the divorce (or even from the costs of a new marriage); freedom to travel (by bus, taxi or even your own car) back and forth between your friends' houses and parents' houses without always having to rely on them for rides.

Obviously, money comes from a finite number of places: a part-time job, pocket money for household chores and gifts from relatives. Carefully explore all of your options and start saving ASAP.

Getting a Job

If you're big into sports or involved with some other activity that takes up most of your after-school time, it may be hard to find room in your life for a job. But if you can make the time, earning an income can be liberating. The minimum legal working age in Britain is 13, and that's only for a paper round. Once you are 15 you can get a job working in a shop or restaurant. But even if you are younger than 13, there are still plenty of jobs you can do. Everybody loves a bargain, and an eager teen offering reasonably-priced services will often get a resounding 'yes!' from neighbours too busy, or too lazy, to do the work themselves. Consider jobs such as mowing lawns, raking leaves, washing cars, walking dogs and babysitting (just make sure you know and trust the people you are working for). And don't forget, having two sets of households gives you two neighbourhoods to offer your services.

Doing Chores for Pocket Money

If you are not already receiving pocket money based on chores, propose this plan to your parents. You don't need transport to do chores around the house, and it's a good way to earn extra money. All parents are thrilled to have help at home; they may secretly wish their kids would volunteer the work out of sheer love and adoration, but in reality, they're often willing to pay for the assistance. And once again, two households equals two sources of income. Ker-ching!

If you can get it to work,
each parent will give you
pocket money – double
the money and
double the fun.

You don't have to take out the rubbish or hoover the living room to score a few extra pounds – though those things are always needed. You can also be creative about what tasks you offer to take on. For example, if one parent is a primary school teacher, you can offer to help mark some spelling tests. If another parent is a carpenter, offer to help with woodcutting or even simple book-keeping. Make a list of what you could do around the house to generate some cash, and present your ideas to your parents.

A couple of years after my parents split up, I decided I needed some money. So I told both of them that I needed to start earning some pocket money. I agreed to do some weekly chores around both houses, and so I got two lots of pocket money. Neither parent gave me a lot of chores to do because I was only at each house for half of the time, but they both gave me the full amount – two for the work of one!

When negotiating how much you should be paid, start higher (within reason) than you think you can get. This way, you have room to negotiate if your parents offer you less – which, let's face it, they probably will. Agree on pay days, too. You may prefer to have a different pay day in each household, depending on what kind of spender you are. If you can't seem to keep money in your pockets, it may be better getting paid on a different day at each house – perhaps Saturdays at your Mum's and Tuesdays at your Dad's – so all your cash doesn't vanish over the weekend. If you usually need bigger amounts of cash for fewer things (perhaps you tend to buy one new piece of clothing at a time, or to go out on one date each week), try to get paid on the same day, or as close together as possible.

Getting to Work

Before you apply for a job, assess the transport situation. If you can walk, cycle or take the bus, great. If not, you may need your parents to take you to work and pick you up. Make sure they know this and agree to do it. You won't have a job for long if you can't get there!

Saving Up for a Car

The ultimate freedom, if you live in a split family, may come in the form of your very own car – and that costs a lot of money. Saving up for a car is a goal that you can achieve through hard work over a summer or two, and it may have a dramatic effect on your quality of life. Few teens would say 'no' to a car, but if you're spending half your life in transit you may be willing to work a little harder for one.

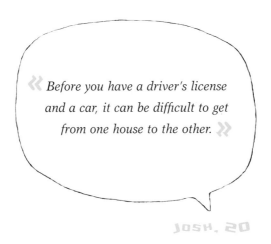

Before you have a driver's license and a car, it can be difficult to get from one house to the other.

JOSH, 20

There's no better time to bring up the subject than when you're being a mature, responsible young man or woman, trying to earn a respectable income. When you approach your parents on this subject, have a plan in place. Are you asking them if they'll allow you to buy a car? Maybe to pay for half? Do you have a particular car in mind? See the negotiation tips in Chapter 2 and start the negotiation armed with the following phrases:

"Used is fine."

"I'll pay for X, Y and Z."

"I'd be happy to drive (insert annoying younger sibling's name here) to clarinet lessons."

"I'll never ask you for anything again. Ever." (No parent will believe this one, but it's worth a try.)

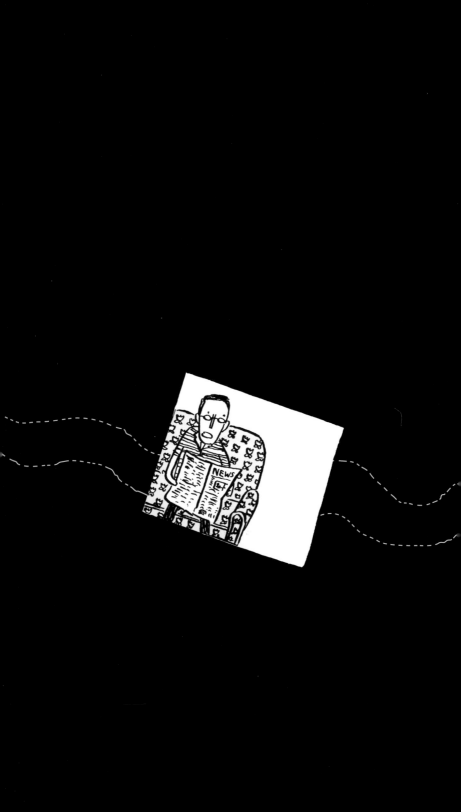

Parent Patrol

Keeping the Adults on Track

Part of the reason you feel disorganised or out of control at times may simply be because your parents are not on the same page as you, your siblings or each other. Your Mum thinks you mean one thing, while your Dad's understanding is totally different. For example, your Mum is sure that taking you to football is your Dad's responsibility, while your Dad is sure that it was something your Mum agreed to do. That leaves you stuck in the middle of an argument – and stuck without a lift.

Everyone has different schedules, priorities and life dramas, and this lack of unity is further complicated if your parents are not on good speaking terms. But all hope is not lost. Even if your parents are big fans of "My house, my rules," or "Not while you're under this roof," they may still accept (and even want) some guidance from you about how to make your travelling lifestyle work. Remember, this situation is not what they were planning either, and they don't always have the answers. Mistakes will be made, and not necessarily admitted. Try to remember that your parents are human, and give them some direction when they need it.

Whose Job Is It Anyway?

You may feel like an adult – and in many ways you are – but in the end you are still living with your parents, and you rely on them for certain things. It's important that all parties know their responsibilities, and it may be up to you to get that discussion going. Talk to your parents about the things you need, and try to make some joint decisions about who is responsible for what. You can have an informal conversation, pass around an e-mail checklist or draw up a contract that you ask them to sign. Regardless of how you approach the situation, keep a record of what your Mum and Dad have agreed to do. This way, if you are ever the recipient of "Your mother said she was going!" or "Wasn't your father

supposed to give you that?" you'll have some evidence to settle the dispute.

1. School and after school

A lot of routine things come up during the school year that require the involvement of one or both of your parents. These basic responsibilities should be sorted out between the three of you, so you know who goes to parent's evenings, who signs your reports and who does whatever else that needs to be done. It's possible that your parents may decide to share some of the tasks listed below; it's also possible that each parent will take on sole responsibility for certain things. Either way, you all need to know that everything is covered – and who is responsible for what.

Ask your parents:

Who goes to parent's evenings?

Who goes to/takes you to school functions (plays, concerts, etc...)?

Who signs your report?

Who goes to your games, matches and ceremonies?

Who takes you to music lessons, sports training and after-school clubs?

BEST
(& WORST)

*Split-in-Two
Moments*

ZOLA, 14

*Once I went on a
Sunday trip with
my Dad and his
partner. On the
drive back there
was a lot of traffic and
therefore the journey was
very slow. I was planning to
cram in a project that night at my
Mum's house that was due in the next
day. However, I had to sleep over at my Dad's
house and rush my project. I took the train to
my Mum's house in the morning. I was late for
school and got into trouble with my teacher.*

2. Money

This is one of the biggest things married couples argue
about, and that often doesn't change when they split up.
Of course, your parents might be the smoothest
dealmakers ever and split everything down the middle.
Or not. If they are not so great with money matters,
it can help to have a discussion with them about this
stuff to make it clear whom you should be relying on
for what. If a discussion is out of the question, consider
sending around a spreadsheet in an e-mail.

Ask your parents:

Who pays for sports equipment?

Who pays for school photographs?

Who pays for school trips?

Who pays for school discos (including the dress or suit)?

Who pays for school lunches?

Who pays for school clothes?

Who pays for your out-of-school activities (dance lessons, art classes, piano lessons, etc...)?

Who pays for your mobile phone?

3. Emergencies and problems at school

You and your parents may have sorted out the basic logistics, but what about more stressful circumstances, such as emergencies or problems at school? For these situations, you might want to have some say over who should be contacted for what. If Mum totally freaks out when you hurt yourself, you might want your school to call your Dad if you injure yourself playing sport. And if Dad will never let you out again if you get that one-time 'D' in maths, put your Mum's number down when your teachers collect your parent/guardian info.

Look at the categories below and decide which parent you want to take care of what, and then check with them to make sure it's cool. (For each situation that involves school, make sure your teachers have the contact info you want them to have.)

• If you get in trouble at school

• If you get hurt at school

• If you get sick at school

• If you're having problems with someone in your class

• If you miss the bus and need a ride

• If you need a ride home from a party where everyone has been drinking

> *I was so proud of the way my Dad handled the duties of raising us when he was single. He had to adapt quickly. He would make our lunches, cook us dinners and help us with our homework. He wasn't the best cook, but he made some great macaroni cheese.* ≫

JEFF, 24

When Parents Go Astray

Splitting up can leave your parents a little off-kilter. One or both of them may be angry at the other, making it difficult for them to communicate about anything, including you. You may even find that when they talk to you, they can't stop themselves from criticising the other parent. Although working together should be their focus, they may slip up at times. Here are some basic things you should request of them.

1. Say only nice things about each other

The last thing you want to hear is that your Dad is always late and can't handle his responsibilities, or that your Mum refuses to listen to anyone. No matter how true this may be, parent-to-parent insults have no place within your earshot. Let your Mum and Dad know that it bothers you to hear them say mean things about each other, and gently ask them to stop.

« *Remember that it is probably better that your parents are divorced than stuck in an unhealthy marriage. But do not fall prey to pressure to pick a favourite.* »

MICA, 17

2. Don't use you as their messenger

If your parents aren't speaking to each other, they may rely on you to do their talking for them. But that is not your responsibility. And when one of them doesn't like what the other one relays through you, guess who has to deal with that? You. Whether the news is good or bad, urgent or not particularly pressing, your parents need to communicate directly with each other, and not through you. If they are struggling with this, kindly suggest that they use e-mail. For scheduling, they can always resort to a web-based calendar system (see page 55).

3. Leave interrogations to the cop shows

Parents are just as insecure as kids, and kids tend to find this out when their parents split up. Suddenly, you may notice that your Mum or Dad is barraging you with question after question about the other parent – the other parent's new spouse, the partner's children or financial situation – you get the picture. Let your parents know you feel uncomfortable talking about them behind their backs.

« Give it time. You'll all
get used to the new
situation. »

EMILY, 15

« You may not have any hope
at the beginning – I know I
didn't – but things will get
better. It just takes time. »

SOPHIE, 17

The Golden Rules (or Lack Thereof)

One of the things that changes the most when your parents split up is the set of rules governing your existence. For some kids, this is totally annoying. It's confusing when Dad says you should be home by 9pm but Mum says 10pm, or when Dad requires you to start homework right after school but Mum never even asks if you have homework. If you feel like you're floundering a little, try to get your parents to agree on basic rules for things such as chores, homework, what time you need to be home and how much pocket money you get. This way, you won't have to adjust to a new set of rules each time you move households.

On the other hand, some teens say that the best part of having divorced parents is that you get two different sets of rules. After all, if Mum is willing to let you stay out later, you can plan to go out with that new boy or girl the next time you stay at her house.

❝ Whatever my Mum doesn't let me do at her house, I get to do at my Dad's – and vice versa. ❞

DANI, 16

At Mum's house, I am allowed to play computer games for hours, while I have to do all my homework first at Dad's. So I end up getting all my homework done at my Dad's house and never finishing it at my Mum's. Although I prefer to be at my Mum's house, my schoolwork and grades suffer because of it.

WESLEY, 15

Now What?

Moving Forward with Your Life

So now, you've learned some good ways to manage your day-to-day, split-living life a little better. But you know, better than anyone, that it's all easier said than done. Living in two homes will still be stressful at times – even if you have the most cooperative parents in the world.

Like any difficult situation, this one calls for patience and a certain willingness to make it work. The mindset with which you approach your split-family life will be one of the main factors determining how successful it will be. Of course, even the most patient, positive person in the world can't make every situation work, so it's also possible that there will come a time when you need to ask for a change.

Look At the Bright Side

If things are working out, great. But when they're not, you can easily get depressed about your situation. If you are feeling down, you're likely to start listing all of the negative things about your circumstances. During these moments of frustration, try to make a list of all of the good things that have come about – or could potentially come about – because your parents don't live together.

For example, maybe you have the opportunity to spend more time with each parent now than you did when they were married. Or maybe you have more independence, more peace and quiet or great new siblings that you wouldn't otherwise have had.

If you are in trouble with one parent, you can always stay with the other. Also, there's always different food in the fridge.

ELI, 18

One advantage to my parents being separated is that I get each parent's own objective advice, which is so much more real and helpful when the other parent is not around.

MAX, 16

If you're about to have a new step-parent, there could also be upsides. It might mean an extra car available to get you where you need to go or another person to help with your homework. If one parent is clingy and wants to know every detail of your life, having a live-in distraction to occupy his or her time could give you more breathing space. And if your relationship with one parent isn't completely perfect at the moment, a new parental unit could fill the gap.

Making a list of what's good about your split-living situation is not meant to dismiss your real concerns; it's simply meant to remind you that things are not *all* bad. And everyone, in any challenging situation, needs to remind themselves of that from time to time.

> *Having two houses gives you more options. Say, for example, you really want to have some time by yourself; you have more options and thus more chances of having an empty house. Say one house stays really cool in the summer and one really warm in the winter. Then you get the best of both worlds.*

JOSH, 20

Requesting a Change

If you've done all that you can do to make the situation work and you are still feeling unhappy, you may want to re-examine your living situation. Not every custody arrangement will succeed. People change, households change, parents move on. Sometimes the situation never really works in the first place. Perhaps too much travelling back and forth interferes with doing your homework or your social life. Or, if you change households weekly, you may miss your other parent while you're away. Or maybe you don't like constantly moving between two houses and believe it's in your best interest to stay at one house and only have day visits with the other parent.

Now that I've left school and living full-time with my Dad – instead of switching houses every other day like I did before – it's a lot easier. I talk to both parents every day on the phone and tell them what I am doing, and as long as I spend a few hours with them once a week, they are fine.

KELSEY, 19

If you decide to talk to your parents about a change, be clear on what's not working – and offer solutions. It might help to go back to Chapter 1 and revisit the various living arrangements to see which ones you think might work better for you than your current situation, and look at the negotiation skills in Chapter 2.

Custody arrangements can change – it happens all the time. But don't expect it to happen overnight. If your parents do agree to adopt a new plan, it may take them a little time to sort out the details and come to terms with the new arrangement. Also consider trying a temporary change – for one month, perhaps – to see if a different arrangement really is the answer. After a month, you may decide that you liked things better the way they were before.

It takes time to get used to a change, and even though it may be rough in the beginning, it gets easier. You get into a routine and you stick with it. Just hang in there and know that, sooner or later, you will feel happier and stronger.

AMANDA, 16

Life Goes On

You may stay in the same living situation until you leave school, or your arrangements may change several times over the years. Either way, you'll find your own ways of dealing with the chaos – and may even learn to like it. Kids from split families often become more adventurous, independent and adaptable adults. And while your life might feel like a bit of a struggle now, those qualities will be really valuable later on.

In the meantime, work towards making the situation as good as it can possibly be. And when all else fails, remember: You won't be living at home forever!

« *I used to wish that my parents had stayed together until I moved away for university, so I could have skipped all the pain I experienced at school. But then I realised that if they had stayed together for my sake, my home life would have been a lie. Now that I am older, I am grateful my parents got divorced. Getting a divorce allowed them to lead happier lives, and I now know that it's worked out better for me.* »

JEFF, 24